Ninja Blast Portable Blender Recipe Book

101 Recipes From Smoothies To Baby Foods

Ramona Caldwell

Copyright © by Ramona Caldwell

All Rights Reserved. No part of this publication may be reproduced, stored in a retrieval system or transmitted, in any form or by any means— electronic, mechanical, photocopying, recording or otherwise- without prior written permission from the publisher, except for the inclusion of brief quotations in a review.

TABLE OF CONTENTS

- INTRODUCTION 6
- BENEFITS OF USING A PORTABLE BLENDER 7
- TIPS FOR MAKING THE PERFECT BLEND 8
- HOW TO CLEAN AND MAINTAIN YOUR NINJA BLAST BLENDER 9
- ENERGIZING BREAKFAST SMOOTHIES 10
  1. Rise & Shine Banana Oat Smoothie 10
  2. Blueberry Almond Boost 10
  3. Tropical Sunrise (Mango & Pineapple) 10
  4. Cinnamon Apple Pie Smoothie 10
  5. Peanut Butter Banana Dream 11
  6. Berry Protein Morning Smoothie 11
  7. Chia Seed Energy Smoothie 11
  8. Green Matcha Morning Kick 11
  9. Maple Walnut Power Shake 11
  10. Carrot Ginger Zing 12
- NUTRITIOUS GREEN SMOOTHIES 12
  11. Classic Green Detox 12
  12. Spinach & Avocado Cream Smoothie 12
  13. Pineapple Kale Refresh 12
  14. Cucumber Mint Green Juice 12
  15. Superfood Spirulina Smoothie 13
  16. Cilantro Lime Detox Smoothie 13
  17. Parsley Power Smoothie 13
  18. Matcha Green Tea Revive 13
  19. Celery Cleanser 13
  20. Mango Green Balance 14
- PROTEIN SHAKES & MUSCLE BUILDERS 14
  21. Chocolate Peanut Power Shake 14
  22. Strawberry Almond Protein Shake 14
  23. Tropical Plant-Based Power Shake 14
  24. Mocha Banana Muscle Builder 14
  25. Vanilla Cinnamon Recovery Shake 15
  26. Peanut Butter Chocolate Energy Boost 15
  27. Pumpkin Spice Protein Shake 15
  28. Oatmeal Cookie Shake 15
  29. Choco-Coconut Power Drink 15
  30. Almond Butter Berry Bliss 16

WEIGHT LOSS DRINKS 16

- 31. GREEN APPLE DETOX 16
- 32. GRAPEFRUIT MINT REFRESHER 16
- 33. METABOLISM BOOSTING BERRY BLAST 16
- 34. CUCUMBER LEMON SLIM SMOOTHIE 16
- 35. FAT-BURNING PINEAPPLE GINGER 17
- 36. SPICY GREEN TEA BLEND 17
- 37. BLUEBERRY ANTIOXIDANT CLEANSER 17
- 38. APPLE CIDER SLIM TONIC 17
- 39. GREEN GRAPES & SPINACH BOOST 17
- 40. CINNAMON PEAR SLIM DOWN 18

LIGHT & REFRESHING JUICES 18

- 41. WATERMELON MINT SPLASH 18
- 42. ORANGE CARROT GLOW 18
- 43. POMEGRANATE PUNCH 18
- 44. TROPICAL CITRUS REFRESH 18
- 45. STRAWBERRY LIME BREEZE 19
- 46. KIWI CUCUMBER COOLER 19
- 47. PEACH LEMON SPRITZ 19
- 48. APPLE CELERY GREEN JUICE 19
- 49. MELON BERRY REFRESHER 19
- 50. CRANBERRY LIME ZEST 20

COFFEES & LATTES 20

- 51. ICED VANILLA LATTE 20
- 52. MOCHA COCONUT BLAST 20
- 53. CINNAMON SPICED COLD BREW 20
- 54. CARAMEL ESPRESSO SMOOTHIE 20
- 55. PUMPKIN SPICE LATTE 21
- 56. ALMOND MOCHA DELIGHT 21
- 57. MATCHA GREEN TEA LATTE 21
- 58. VANILLA ALMOND LATTE 21
- 59. CLASSIC COLD BREW 21
- 60. HONEY CINNAMON ICED COFFEE 22

SALAD DRESSINGS 22

- 61. CLASSIC BALSAMIC VINAIGRETTE 22
- 62. CREAMY CAESAR DRESSING 22
- 63. ZESTY ITALIAN DRESSING 22
- 64. GREEK YOGURT RANCH 22
- 65. LEMON TAHINI DRESSING 23
- 66. AVOCADO LIME DRESSING 23
- 67. HONEY MUSTARD VINAIGRETTE 23
- 68. MANGO CILANTRO DRESSING 23
- 69. GREEN GODDESS SMOOTHIE DRESSING 23
- 70. CHIPOTLE LIME DRESSING 24

KIDS SMOOTHIES 24
71. Chocolate Banana Bliss 24
72. Blueberry Burst 24
73. Strawberry Vanilla Twist 24
74. Tropical Pineapple Punch 24
75. Orange Cream Dream 25
76. Peanut Butter Banana Pop 25
77. Apple Pie Smoothie 25
78. Watermelon Wonder 25
79. Raspberry Lemonade Twist 25
80. Cherry Berry Explosion 26

MILKSHAKES 26
81. Classic Vanilla Bean Milkshake 26
82. Chocolate Fudge Milkshake 26
83. Peanut Butter Cup Shake 26
84. Cookies & Cream Delight 26
85. Strawberry Cheesecake Shake 27
86. Salted Caramel Crunch 27
87. Mint Chocolate Chip Shake 27
88. Banana Split Milkshake 27
89. Pistachio Dream Shake 27
90. Espresso Brownie Blast 28

BABY FOOD 28
91. Banana Pear Puree 28
92. Sweet Potato Carrot Mash 28
93. Apple Avocado Smoothie 28
94. Peach Mango Puree 28
95. Butternut Squash Delight 29
96. Carrot Spinach Blend 29
97. Blueberry Oatmeal Puree 29
98. Pea & Pear Puree 29
99. Mango & Banana Bliss 29
100. Zucchini & Apple Mix 30
101. Sweet Potato Pumpkin Mash 30

INTRODUCTION

I'm so excited to share these 101 amazing recipes with you! Whether you're looking to boost your morning routine, refuel after a workout, or prepare something quick and delicious for the family, this book has it all. The Ninja Blast Portable Blender is not just convenient—it's powerful enough to whip up smooth, delicious blends wherever you are. It's perfect for busy mornings, post-gym protein shakes, and even making baby food on the go.

Here's what you can expect from this book:

Simple, Fast Recipes: These recipes are designed to be quick and easy. No need for fancy ingredients or long prep times—just toss everything in, blend, and enjoy!

Balanced Nutrition: Every recipe is crafted to help you reach your health goals. From energizing smoothies to protein-packed shakes and weight loss drinks, there's something for everyone.

On-the-Go Convenience: With the Ninja Blast, you can blend wherever life takes you. From your kitchen counter to your office desk, or even the gym, it's your personal blender ready to go!

This book is all about making life easier, tastier, and healthier. No matter what your schedule looks like, you'll have a variety of flavorful options at your fingertips. I hope you find recipes that become your new favorites, and that they make healthy eating a breeze for you and your family.

Let's get blending!

BENEFITS OF USING A PORTABLE BLENDER

A portable blender like the Ninja Blast isn't just another kitchen gadget—it's a game changer for anyone who loves convenience without sacrificing health and nutrition. Here's why it's such a powerful tool to have in your daily routine:

1. **Ultimate Convenience:** No need to be stuck in the kitchen to make your favorite drinks or snacks. With a portable blender, you can blend up a smoothie, shake, or juice anywhere—whether you're at home, in the office, at the gym, or even on the road. Its compact size makes it easy to carry in a bag or backpack.
2. **Healthy Eating, Anytime, Anywhere:** Eating healthy can sometimes feel like a hassle, especially when you're out and about. With a portable blender, you can make fresh, nutritious meals and snacks on the go. Blend a quick protein shake after your workout or prepare a smoothie during a lunch break. It's all about maintaining a healthy lifestyle no matter where you are.
3. **Quick Clean-Up:** Cleaning a full-sized blender can be a chore. A portable blender, on the other hand, is designed for easy clean-up. Most models are dishwasher-safe, and because they're smaller, you can simply rinse out the cup and blade right after use, saving you a lot of time and hassle.
4. **Save Time & Money:** Instead of spending money on store-bought smoothies, juices, or shakes, you can create them yourself with fresh ingredients in just minutes. Plus, you'll know exactly what's going into your drinks—no hidden sugars or preservatives. It's not only better for your body but also for your wallet.
5. **Customizable Recipes:** A portable blender gives you the flexibility to experiment with different ingredients and tailor your recipes to fit your dietary needs or taste preferences. You can create everything from green detox smoothies to indulgent milkshakes, all in one device.
6. **Perfect Portion Control:** Full-sized blenders often make large batches, but with a portable blender, you're getting the ideal single-serving size. This helps with portion control, preventing waste, and ensuring that you're making just the right amount for yourself (or even a little one, when it comes to baby food).
7. **Blend Anywhere, Anytime:** Many portable blenders are rechargeable and don't need to be plugged in during use, meaning you can blend literally anywhere—from camping trips to beach days or even during your commute. It's like having a personal chef with you at all times.
8. **Versatile Usage:** While smoothies might be the first thing that comes to mind, a portable blender can do so much more. You can whip up protein shakes, baby food, salad dressings, sauces, and even frozen cocktails! It's a versatile tool that opens up endless possibilities.

TIPS FOR MAKING THE PERFECT BLEND

Blending the perfect smoothie, shake, or juice doesn't just come down to throwing ingredients into your portable blender. With a few smart tips, you can take your blends from good to absolutely amazing! Here's how to make sure every time you blend, you're getting the best texture, flavor, and nutrition possible:

1. **Start with Liquids First:** Always add your liquids at the bottom of the blender. This creates a smooth base for the blades to move and prevents the ingredients from getting stuck. Whether it's water, juice, milk, or yogurt, this step ensures that your ingredients blend evenly.
2. **Cut Ingredients into Small Pieces:** Even though portable blenders are powerful, it helps to chop your fruits, veggies, and other ingredients into smaller pieces. This reduces blending time and gives you a smoother result. Plus, smaller pieces are easier on the blender's motor, prolonging its life.
3. **Layer Ingredients for Best Results:** The order of ingredients can make a big difference in the consistency of your blend. Here's a layering rule of thumb for perfect texture:
4. **Liquids first (as mentioned above):**
    - Soft ingredients like yogurt, banana, or avocado
    - Frozen fruits and ice go next
    - Hard ingredients (seeds, nuts, or leafy greens) on top
5. **Don't Overfill:** It might be tempting to pack everything in, but resist the urge! Overfilling the blender can lead to uneven blending and messes when the contents overflow. Fill it about three-quarters full to give the blades space to move freely and ensure an even blend.
6. **Pulse, Then Blend:** For a smoother blend, start by pulsing the ingredients a few times. This helps break down larger chunks and gets everything moving before you go full blend. Pulsing can also help prevent air pockets from forming around the blades.
7. **Use Frozen Fruit for a Thicker Texture:** If you want a thick, frosty smoothie without using ice (which can water down your drink), opt for frozen fruit. It adds a rich, creamy texture and keeps your drink cold and refreshing. Bonus: Frozen fruits often maintain their nutrients better than fresh fruit sitting out for days.
8. **Add Greens Gradually:** Green smoothies are a great way to pack in extra nutrients, but too many leafy greens can overpower the flavor and make the texture gritty. Start by adding a handful of spinach, kale, or other greens, and blend. If needed, add more gradually until you find your perfect balance.
9. **Adjust the Thickness:** If your blend comes out too thick or too thin, it's easy to fix:
    - Too thick? Add a splash of liquid (water, milk, juice) and blend again.
    - Too thin? Throw in more frozen fruit, ice, or yogurt to thicken it up.
10. **Balance Your Flavors:** For a perfectly balanced smoothie, make sure you're hitting a mix of:
    - Sweetness from fruits like bananas, mangos, or berries
    - Creaminess from yogurt, milk, or avocado
    - Tartness from citrus fruits or a dash of lemon juice
    - Freshness from greens, cucumber, or herbs like mint
11. **Don't Forget the Protein & Healthy Fats:** To make your smoothies more filling and nutritious, add sources of protein and healthy fats. Options like nut butters, chia seeds, Greek yogurt, or protein powder will help keep you fuller for longer and add a creamy texture.
12. **Add Boosts for Extra Nutrition:** Supercharge your blend by adding a nutrient boost! A tablespoon of flax seeds or chia seeds adds fiber and healthy fats, while a scoop of spirulina or protein powder can give your smoothie that extra nutritional punch.
13. **Blend Longer for a Smoother Texture:** Sometimes, impatience leads to chunky smoothies. Let your blender run for a little longer—an extra 20-30 seconds—to ensure all the ingredients are fully combined and you're left with a silky-smooth drink.
14. **Taste and Adjust Before Serving:** Before pouring out your blend, give it a taste. Too tart? Add a little honey or maple syrup. Too sweet? Add more greens or a splash of lemon. Adjust the flavor to your liking before you serve it.

How to Clean and Maintain Your Ninja Blast Blender

Taking good care of your Ninja Blast portable blender will keep it performing at its best and help it last longer. Fortunately, cleaning and maintaining this blender is quick and easy if you follow a few simple steps. Here's how to keep it in top shape after each use:

Rinse Immediately After Use:
As soon as you're done blending, give your Ninja Blast a quick rinse. This helps prevent food or smoothie residue from sticking to the blades and walls of the cup. Just add some warm water and a drop of dish soap, then blend for a few seconds before rinsing it out.

Disassemble for a Thorough Clean:
For a deeper clean, disassemble the blender by separating the cup, blade assembly, and base (if possible). This lets you clean each part individually, ensuring no hidden residue is left behind. Most parts are designed to be easily removed, making it hassle-free.

Use a Soft Sponge or Brush:
When washing the blender parts by hand, avoid using abrasive sponges or steel wool. These can scratch the surfaces or damage the blades. Instead, use a soft sponge or a small brush to gently scrub the cup, blades, and other parts.

Pay Special Attention to the Blades:
The blades do the hard work, so they need special care. Clean around the blades carefully to remove any stuck-on food or fiber. Be cautious when handling them, as they're sharp. A small cleaning brush or toothbrush works well for reaching tight spots around the blades.

Dishwasher-Safe Components:
Many Ninja Blast components are dishwasher-safe (check the user manual for confirmation). Place the blender cup, lid, and blades on the top rack of your dishwasher for a hands-off clean. Just be sure to avoid putting the motor base in the dishwasher, as it contains electrical components.

Clean the Base with a Damp Cloth:
For the motor base, never submerge it in water. Instead, use a damp cloth to wipe it down. If any smoothie spills or splashes occur on the base, wipe them up immediately to prevent buildup. Make sure the base is dry before using the blender again.

Remove Stubborn Odors or Stains:
Over time, certain ingredients like turmeric or beets might leave stains or odors in the blender cup. To get rid of these, blend a mixture of baking soda and water or a splash of vinegar with water. Let it sit for a few minutes, then rinse thoroughly. This will deodorize and help lift any lingering stains.

Check for Wear and Tear:
Regularly inspect your blender's parts, especially the blades and seals. If you notice the blades becoming dull or the rubber seals wearing out, you may need to replace these parts. Keeping everything in good condition will ensure your blender continues to work efficiently.

Recharge Regularly:
Make sure to keep your Ninja Blast's battery charged. Check the charging indicator lights regularly, and try not to let it drain completely before recharging. Most portable blenders come with a USB charging port, so you can easily charge it using any USB power source. A well-maintained battery will keep your blender running smoothly when you need it.

Avoid Overfilling:
To avoid unnecessary strain on your blender, never fill it above the maximum fill line. Overfilling can cause the motor to overwork, leading to potential damage and poor blending results. Stick to the recommended amount of ingredients for the best performance.

Store It Properly:
When you're not using your Ninja Blast, store it in a cool, dry place. Make sure all parts are clean and dry before putting them away. This prevents the growth of mold or mildew, especially on any rubber seals or hard-to-reach areas.

ENERGIZING BREAKFAST SMOOTHIES

1. Rise & Shine Banana Oat Smoothie

Prep Time: 5 minutes | Serve: 1

Ingredients

- 1 ripe banana
- ½ cup rolled oats
- 1 cup almond milk (or milk of choice)
- 1 tsp honey or maple syrup (optional)
- ¼ tsp cinnamon
- Ice cubes (optional)

Instructions

1. First, press the Power Button on your Ninja Blast Portable Blender.
2. Add the banana, oats, almond milk, honey (if you like it a bit sweeter), and cinnamon to the blender cup.
3. Pop in a few ice cubes if you want a chilled smoothie.
4. Secure the lid, then press the Start/Stop Button to blend until smooth, about 30–45 seconds.
5. Pour into your favorite glass, sip, and enjoy your energizing breakfast boost!

2. Blueberry Almond Boost

Prep Time: 5 minutes | Serve: 1

Ingredients

- 1 cup fresh or frozen blueberries
- ½ cup plain Greek yogurt
- ½ cup almond milk
- 1 tbsp almond butter
- 1 tsp honey or agave syrup (optional)
- A few ice cubes for extra chill

Instructions

1. Power up your Ninja Blast Portable Blender.
2. Add the blueberries, Greek yogurt, almond milk, almond butter, and honey to the blender cup.
3. Toss in some ice cubes if you like it cold.
4. Secure the lid, then press the Start/Stop Button to blend until creamy, about 45 seconds.
5. Pour into a glass and enjoy a protein-packed morning boost!

3. Tropical Sunrise (Mango & Pineapple)

Prep Time: 5 minutes | Serve: 1

Ingredients

- ½ cup frozen mango chunks
- ½ cup frozen pineapple chunks
- 1 cup coconut water
- ½ tsp chia seeds (optional for added nutrients)

Instructions

1. Start by turning on your Ninja Blast Portable Blender.
2. Add the mango, pineapple, and coconut water to the blender cup.
3. If you'd like a nutrient boost, sprinkle in the chia seeds.
4. Secure the lid, then press Start/Stop and blend until smooth, about 30–45 seconds.
5. Pour into a glass, close your eyes, and imagine you're in paradise!

4. Cinnamon Apple Pie Smoothie

Prep Time: 5 minutes | Serve: 1

Ingredients

- 1 apple, cored and sliced
- ½ cup Greek yogurt
- 1 cup almond milk (or milk of choice)
- ¼ tsp cinnamon
- 1 tsp honey (optional)
- Ice cubes (optional)

Instructions

1. Press the Power Button to start up your blender.
2. Add the apple slices, Greek yogurt, almond milk, cinnamon, and honey to the blender cup.
3. Add ice cubes if you want it extra chilled.
4. Press Start/Stop to blend for 30–45 seconds until it's smooth.
5. Pour into a glass and enjoy a smoothie that tastes like a delicious apple pie!

5. Peanut Butter Banana Dream

Prep Time: 5 minutes | Serve: 1

Ingredients
- 1 banana
- 1 tbsp peanut butter
- 1 cup milk (any type works)
- 1 tbsp rolled oats
- A few ice cubes (optional)

Instructions
1. Power up your Ninja Blast Portable Blender.
2. Place the banana, peanut butter, milk, and oats in the blender cup.
3. Add ice cubes if you want it colder.
4. Press Start/Stop to blend until it's creamy, about 30–45 seconds.
5. Pour into a glass, take a sip, and feel the creamy, nutty goodness kickstart your day!

6. Berry Protein Morning Smoothie

Prep Time: 5 minutes | Serve: 1

Ingredients
1 cup mixed berries (fresh or frozen)

- ½ cup Greek yogurt
- 1 cup milk (any kind you like)
- 1 tbsp chia seeds (optional for added protein)
- Ice cubes (optional)

Instructions
1. Turn on your Ninja Blast Portable Blender by pressing the Power Button.
2. Add berries, Greek yogurt, milk, and chia seeds to the blender cup.
3. Add ice cubes if you want a cooler drink.
4. Press Start/Stop and blend until smooth, about 45 seconds.
5. Pour into a glass and enjoy the burst of berry flavors!

7. Chia Seed Energy Smoothie

Prep Time: 5 minutes | Serve: 1

Ingredients
- 1 banana
- 1 tbsp chia seeds
- 1 cup almond milk
- 1 tsp honey (optional)
- A few ice cubes

Instructions
1. Power up your Ninja Blast Portable Blender.
2. Add the banana, chia seeds, almond milk, and honey to the blender.
3. Pop in some ice cubes if you like it chilled.
4. Press Start/Stop to blend until smooth, about 45 seconds.
5. Pour into a glass and sip on this energy-boosting smoothie!

8. Green Matcha Morning Kick

Prep Time: 5 minutes | Serve: 1

Ingredients
- 1 tsp matcha powder
- 1 banana
- ½ cup spinach
- 1 cup almond milk
- ½ tsp honey (optional)

Instructions
1. Start by pressing the Power Button on your Ninja Blast Portable Blender.
2. Add matcha powder, banana, spinach, almond milk, and honey to the blender cup.
3. Secure the lid, press Start/Stop, and blend until creamy, about 45 seconds.
4. Pour into a glass and feel the matcha magic kickstart your day!

9. Maple Walnut Power Shake

Prep Time: 5 minutes | Serve: 1

Ingredients
- 1 banana
- 1 tbsp walnut pieces
- 1 cup milk (any type you prefer)
- 1 tsp maple syrup
- Ice cubes (optional)

Instructions
1. Power up your Ninja Blast Portable Blender.
2. Place the banana, walnuts, milk, and maple syrup in the blender cup.
3. Add ice cubes if you want a frosty texture.
4. Press Start/Stop to blend until smooth, about 45 seconds.
5. Pour into a glass and enjoy this nutty, maple-infused shake!

10. Carrot Ginger Zing

Prep Time: 5 minutes | Serve: 1

Ingredients
- 1 small carrot, peeled and chopped
- 1 small piece of fresh ginger (about ½ inch, peeled)
- 1 orange, peeled
- 1 cup coconut water
- Ice cubes (optional)

Instructions
1. Begin by turning on your Ninja Blast Portable Blender.
2. Add carrot, ginger, orange, and coconut water to the blender cup.
3. Toss in ice cubes if you'd like it colder.
4. Press Start/Stop to blend until smooth, about 45 seconds.
5. Pour into a glass and let the refreshing carrot-ginger combo wake you up!

NUTRITIOUS GREEN SMOOTHIES

11. Classic Green Detox

Prep Time: 5 minutes | Serve: 1

Ingredients
- 1 cup spinach
- ½ cucumber, sliced
- 1 green apple, cored and sliced
- ½ lemon, juiced
- 1 cup water
- Ice cubes (optional)

Instructions
1. First, press the Power Button on your Ninja Blast Portable Blender to turn it on.
2. Add the spinach, cucumber, apple, lemon juice, and water to the blender cup.
3. Toss in a few ice cubes if you prefer a chilled drink.
4. Secure the lid and press Start/Stop to blend until smooth, about 30–45 seconds.
5. Pour into a glass and enjoy the refreshing, detoxifying power of greens!

12. Spinach & Avocado Cream Smoothie

Prep Time: 5 minutes | Serve: 1

Ingredients
- 1 cup spinach
- ½ avocado
- 1 cup almond milk (or milk of choice)
- 1 tsp honey (optional)
- Ice cubes (optional)

Instructions
1. Power on your Ninja Blast Portable Blender.
2. Add the spinach, avocado, almond milk, and honey to the blender cup.
3. Add ice cubes if you like a frosty texture.
4. Press Start/Stop to blend until creamy and smooth, about 45 seconds.
5. Pour into a glass and enjoy this rich, nutrient-packed smoothie!

13. Pineapple Kale Refresh

Prep Time: 5 minutes | Serve: 1

Ingredients
- 1 cup kale, stems removed
- ½ cup pineapple chunks (fresh or frozen)
- 1 cup coconut water
- ½ tsp chia seeds (optional)

Instructions
1. Start by turning on your Ninja Blast Portable Blender.
2. Add the kale, pineapple, coconut water, and chia seeds to the blender cup.
3. Secure the lid, press Start/Stop, and blend until smooth, about 30–45 seconds.
4. Pour into a glass and sip on this tropical green treat!

14. Cucumber Mint Green Juice

Prep Time: 5 minutes | Serve: 1

Ingredients
- ½ cucumber, sliced
- 1 handful fresh mint leaves
- 1 green apple, cored and sliced
- 1 cup water
- Ice cubes (optional)

Instructions
1. Turn on your Ninja Blast Portable Blender.
2. Add the cucumber, mint leaves, apple, and water to the blender cup.
3. Add ice cubes if you like it extra cool.
4. Press Start/Stop to blend until smooth, about 45 seconds.
5. Pour into a glass and enjoy this refreshing minty green juice!

15. Superfood Spirulina Smoothie

Prep Time: 5 minutes | Serve: 1

Ingredients
- 1 banana
- 1 cup spinach
- 1 cup almond milk (or milk of choice)
- ½ tsp spirulina powder
- Ice cubes (optional)

Instructions
1. Power up your Ninja Blast Portable Blender.
2. Add the banana, spinach, almond milk, and spirulina powder to the blender cup.
3. Toss in ice cubes if you'd like it cold.
4. Press Start/Stop to blend until creamy and smooth, about 45 seconds.
5. Pour into a glass, and enjoy this nutrient-rich, green superfood smoothie!

16. Cilantro Lime Detox Smoothie

Prep Time: 5 minutes | Serve: 1

Ingredients
- 1 handful fresh cilantro
- ½ cucumber, sliced
- ½ lime, juiced
- 1 cup coconut water
- Ice cubes (optional)

Instructions
1. Start by pressing the Power Button on your Ninja Blast Portable Blender.
2. Add the cilantro, cucumber, lime juice, and coconut water to the blender cup.
3. Add ice cubes if you want it cold.
4. Press Start/Stop to blend until smooth, about 30–45 seconds.
5. Pour into a glass and enjoy the zesty, refreshing detox smoothie!

17. Parsley Power Smoothie

Prep Time: 5 minutes | Serve: 1

Ingredients
- 1 handful fresh parsley
- ½ green apple, cored and sliced
- 1 cup water
- ½ tsp honey (optional)
- Ice cubes (optional)

Instructions
1. Power on your Ninja Blast Portable Blender.
2. Add the parsley, green apple, water, and honey (if you like it sweeter) to the blender cup.
3. Add ice cubes if you want it extra cool.
4. Press Start/Stop to blend until smooth, about 45 seconds.
5. Pour into a glass, sip, and feel the freshness of parsley power up your day!

18. Matcha Green Tea Revive

Prep Time: 5 minutes | Serve: 1

Ingredients
- 1 tsp matcha powder
- ½ banana
- 1 cup almond milk (or milk of choice)
- A handful of spinach
- Ice cubes (optional)

Instructions
1. First, press the Power Button to turn on your Ninja Blast Portable Blender.
2. Add matcha powder, banana, almond milk, and spinach to the blender cup.
3. Toss in some ice cubes if you want it chilled.
4. Press Start/Stop to blend until creamy, about 45 seconds.
5. Pour into a glass and enjoy this energizing green tea smoothie!

19. Celery Cleanser

Prep Time: 5 minutes | Serve: 1

Ingredients
- 1 celery stalk, chopped
- ½ cucumber, sliced
- 1 green apple, cored and sliced
- 1 cup water
- Ice cubes (optional)

Instructions
- Start by powering on your Ninja Blast Portable Blender.
- Add celery, cucumber, apple, and water to the blender cup.
- Add ice cubes if you prefer it cold.
- Press Start/Stop to blend until smooth, about 45 seconds.
- Pour into a glass, and enjoy this refreshing cleanser!

20. Mango Green Balance

Prep Time: 5 minutes | Serve: 1

Ingredients
- 1 cup mango chunks (fresh or frozen)
- 1 handful kale, stems removed
- 1 cup coconut water
- ½ tsp chia seeds (optional)

Instructions
1. Turn on your Ninja Blast Portable Blender by pressing the Power Button.
2. Add mango, kale, coconut water, and chia seeds to the blender cup.
3. Secure the lid and press Start/Stop to blend until smooth, about 30–45 seconds.
4. Pour into a glass and let this delicious mango green smoothie fuel your day!

PROTEIN SHAKES & MUSCLE BUILDERS

21. Chocolate Peanut Power Shake

Prep Time: 5 minutes | Serve: 1

Ingredients
- 1 scoop chocolate protein powder
- 1 tbsp peanut butter
- 1 banana
- 1 cup almond milk (or milk of choice)
- A few ice cubes (optional)

Instructions
1. Press the Power Button to turn on your Ninja Blast Portable Blender.
2. Add the chocolate protein powder, peanut butter, banana, and almond milk to the blender cup.
3. Toss in some ice cubes if you want it extra cold.
4. Secure the lid, then press Start/Stop to blend until smooth, about 30–45 seconds.
5. Pour into a glass, sip, and enjoy the rich chocolate and peanut butter combo!

22. Strawberry Almond Protein Shake

Prep Time: 5 minutes | Serve: 1

Ingredients
- 1 scoop vanilla protein powder
- ½ cup fresh or frozen strawberries
- 1 cup almond milk
- 1 tbsp almond butter
- A few ice cubes (optional)

Instructions
1. Start by turning on your Ninja Blast Portable Blender.
2. Add the protein powder, strawberries, almond milk, and almond butter to the blender cup.
3. Add ice cubes if you'd like it chilled.
4. Secure the lid, then press Start/Stop to blend until smooth, about 45 seconds.
5. Pour into a glass, and enjoy this creamy, protein-packed shake!

23. Tropical Plant-Based Power Shake

Prep Time: 5 minutes | Serve: 1

Ingredients
- 1 scoop plant-based protein powder
- ½ cup pineapple chunks (fresh or frozen)
- ½ cup mango chunks (fresh or frozen)
- 1 cup coconut water
- A few ice cubes (optional)

Instructions
1. Power up your Ninja Blast Portable Blender by pressing the Power Button.
2. Add the protein powder, pineapple, mango, and coconut water to the blender cup.
3. Add ice cubes if you want it colder.
4. Press Start/Stop to blend until smooth, about 45 seconds.
5. Pour into a glass, close your eyes, and enjoy this tropical energy booster!

24. Mocha Banana Muscle Builder

Prep Time: 5 minutes | Serve: 1

Ingredients
- 1 scoop chocolate protein powder
- ½ cup brewed coffee (cooled)
- 1 banana
- ½ cup milk of choice
- A few ice cubes (optional)

Instructions
1. Press the Power Button to turn on your blender.
2. Add the protein powder, coffee, banana, and milk to the blender cup.
3. Pop in some ice cubes if you like it frosty.
4. Press Start/Stop to blend until creamy, about 45 seconds.
5. Pour into a glass and get a tasty caffeine kick along with your protein!

25. Vanilla Cinnamon Recovery Shake

Prep Time: 5 minutes | Serve: 1

Ingredients
- 1 scoop vanilla protein powder
- ½ tsp cinnamon
- 1 banana
- 1 cup almond milk (or milk of choice)
- A few ice cubes (optional)

Instructions
1. Start by pressing the Power Button to turn on your Ninja Blast Portable Blender.
2. Add the protein powder, cinnamon, banana, and almond milk to the blender cup.
3. Add some ice cubes if you want it chilled.
4. Press Start/Stop to blend until smooth, about 45 seconds.
5. Pour into a glass and enjoy the creamy cinnamon goodness!

26. Peanut Butter Chocolate Energy Boost

Prep Time: 5 minutes | Serve: 1

Ingredients
- 1 scoop chocolate protein powder
- 1 tbsp peanut butter
- 1 cup milk of choice
- ½ tsp honey (optional)
- A few ice cubes (optional)

Instructions
1. Power on your Ninja Blast Portable Blender.
2. Add the protein powder, peanut butter, milk, and honey to the blender cup.
3. Add ice cubes if you like it extra cold.
4. Press Start/Stop to blend until creamy and smooth, about 45 seconds.
5. Pour into a glass and enjoy this chocolatey energy boost!

27. Pumpkin Spice Protein Shake

Prep Time: 5 minutes | Serve: 1

Ingredients
- 1 scoop vanilla protein powder
- ½ cup pumpkin puree
- 1 cup almond milk (or milk of choice)
- ½ tsp pumpkin spice mix
- A few ice cubes (optional)

Instructions
1. Turn on your Ninja Blast Portable Blender by pressing the Power Button.
2. Add the protein powder, pumpkin puree, almond milk, and pumpkin spice mix to the blender cup.
3. Add ice cubes if you want it chilled.
4. Press Start/Stop to blend until smooth, about 45 seconds.
5. Pour into a glass and savor the taste of pumpkin spice with a protein twist!

28. Oatmeal Cookie Shake

Prep Time: 5 minutes | Serve: 1

Ingredients
- 1 scoop vanilla protein powder
- 1 tbsp rolled oats
- ½ tsp cinnamon
- 1 cup almond milk
- ½ banana
- A few ice cubes (optional)

Instructions
1. Press the Power Button to turn on your blender.
2. Add the protein powder, oats, cinnamon, almond milk, and banana to the blender cup.
3. Add ice cubes if you like it cold.
4. Press Start/Stop to blend until smooth, about 45 seconds.
5. Pour into a glass and enjoy this delicious, oat-packed shake!

29. Choco-Coconut Power Drink

Prep Time: 5 minutes | Serve: 1

Ingredients
- 1 scoop chocolate protein powder
- 1 cup coconut milk
- 1 tbsp shredded coconut
- A few ice cubes (optional)

Instructions
1. Start by pressing the Power Button on your Ninja Blast Portable Blender.
2. Add the protein powder, coconut milk, and shredded coconut to the blender cup.
3. Add ice cubes if you want it extra chilled.
4. Press Start/Stop to blend until smooth, about 45 seconds.
5. Pour into a glass and savor the tropical chocolate blend!

30. Almond Butter Berry Bliss

Prep Time: 5 minutes | Serve: 1

Ingredients
- 1 scoop vanilla protein powder
- ½ cup mixed berries (fresh or frozen)
- 1 tbsp almond butter
- 1 cup almond milk (or milk of choice)
- A few ice cubes (optional)

Instructions
1. Press the Power Button to turn on your Ninja Blast Portable Blender.
2. Add the protein powder, berries, almond butter, and almond milk to the blender cup.
3. Add ice cubes if you like it cold.
4. Press Start/Stop to blend until smooth, about 45 seconds.
5. Pour into a glass and enjoy this creamy, fruity, almond-buttery bliss!

WEIGHT LOSS DRINKS

31. Green Apple Detox

Prep Time: 5 minutes | Serve: 1

Ingredients
- 1 green apple, cored and sliced
- ½ cucumber, sliced
- 1 cup water
- ½ lemon, juiced
- Ice cubes (optional)

Instructions
1. Start by pressing the Power Button on your Ninja Blast Portable Blender to turn it on.
2. Add the green apple, cucumber, water, and lemon juice to the blender cup.
3. Add ice cubes if you want it extra cold.
4. Press Start/Stop to blend until smooth, about 30–45 seconds.
5. Pour into a glass and enjoy the refreshing detox boost!

32. Grapefruit Mint Refresher

Prep Time: 5 minutes | Serve: 1

Ingredients
- ½ grapefruit, peeled and segmented
- 1 handful fresh mint leaves
- 1 cup water
- 1 tsp honey (optional)
- Ice cubes (optional)

Instructions
1. Power on your Ninja Blast Portable Blender.
2. Add the grapefruit, mint leaves, water, and honey (if you like a touch of sweetness) to the blender cup.
3. Add ice cubes if desired.
4. Press Start/Stop to blend until smooth, about 30–45 seconds.
5. Pour into a glass and enjoy this cooling, zesty drink that's perfect for a slim-down boost!

33. Metabolism Boosting Berry Blast

Prep Time: 5 minutes | Serve: 1

Ingredients
- ½ cup mixed berries (blueberries, raspberries, strawberries)
- 1 cup green tea, chilled
- ½ tsp honey (optional)
- Ice cubes (optional)

Instructions
1. Press the Power Button to turn on your Ninja Blast Portable Blender.
2. Add the mixed berries, green tea, and honey (if desired) to the blender cup.
3. Toss in some ice cubes if you like it cold.
4. Press Start/Stop to blend until smooth, about 45 seconds.
5. Pour into a glass, sip, and let the berry goodness boost your metabolism!

34. Cucumber Lemon Slim Smoothie

Prep Time: 5 minutes | Serve: 1

Ingredients
- ½ cucumber, sliced
- ½ lemon, juiced
- 1 cup water
- A pinch of ginger powder
- Ice cubes (optional)

Instructions
1. Start by pressing the Power Button on your blender.
2. Add the cucumber, lemon juice, water, and ginger powder to the blender cup.
3. Add some ice cubes if you want it extra refreshing.
4. Press Start/Stop to blend until smooth, about 30–45 seconds.
5. Pour into a glass and enjoy this cool, hydrating drink that supports weight loss!

35. Fat-Burning Pineapple Ginger

Prep Time: 5 minutes | Serve: 1

Ingredients
- ½ cup pineapple chunks (fresh or frozen)
- 1 tsp fresh ginger, grated
- 1 cup coconut water
- Ice cubes (optional)

Instructions
1. Press the Power Button to turn on your Ninja Blast Portable Blender.
2. Add the pineapple, ginger, and coconut water to the blender cup.
3. Add some ice cubes if you want it cold.
4. Press Start/Stop to blend until smooth, about 45 seconds.
5. Pour into a glass and enjoy this tropical, fat-burning blend!

36. Spicy Green Tea Blend

Prep Time: 5 minutes | Serve: 1

Ingredients
- 1 cup green tea, chilled
- ½ lemon, juiced
- A pinch of cayenne pepper
- 1 tsp honey (optional)

Instructions
1. Power on your Ninja Blast Portable Blender.
2. Add the green tea, lemon juice, cayenne pepper, and honey (if you want some sweetness) to the blender cup.
3. Secure the lid and press Start/Stop to blend until smooth, about 30 seconds.
4. Pour into a glass and sip on this metabolism-boosting, spicy blend!

37. Blueberry Antioxidant Cleanser

Prep Time: 5 minutes | Serve: 1

Ingredients
- ½ cup blueberries (fresh or frozen)
- 1 cup water
- ½ lemon, juiced
- Ice cubes (optional)

Instructions
1. Start by pressing the Power Button on your blender.
2. Add the blueberries, water, and lemon juice to the blender cup.
3. Add ice cubes if desired.
4. Press Start/Stop to blend until smooth, about 45 seconds.
5. Pour into a glass and enjoy the cleansing power of antioxidant-rich blueberries!

38. Apple Cider Slim Tonic

Prep Time: 5 minutes | Serve: 1

Ingredients
- 1 tbsp apple cider vinegar
- ½ apple, sliced
- 1 cup water
- ½ tsp honey (optional)
- Ice cubes (optional)

Instructions
1. Power up your Ninja Blast Portable Blender.
2. Add the apple cider vinegar, apple slices, water, and honey (if you like it a little sweeter) to the blender cup.
3. Add some ice cubes for extra chill.
4. Press Start/Stop to blend until smooth, about 45 seconds.
5. Pour into a glass and enjoy this tangy, metabolism-boosting tonic!

39. Green Grapes & Spinach Boost

Prep Time: 5 minutes | Serve: 1

Ingredients
- ½ cup green grapes
- 1 handful spinach
- 1 cup water
- A few ice cubes (optional)

Instructions
1. Turn on your Ninja Blast Portable Blender by pressing the Power Button.
2. Add the green grapes, spinach, and water to the blender cup.
3. Add ice cubes if you like it chilled.
4. Press Start/Stop to blend until smooth, about 45 seconds.
5. Pour into a glass, sip, and enjoy this naturally sweet and energizing drink!

40. Cinnamon Pear Slim Down

Prep Time: 5 minutes | Serve: 1

Ingredients
- 1 pear, cored and sliced
- ½ tsp cinnamon
- 1 cup almond milk (or milk of choice)
- Ice cubes (optional)

Instructions
1. Start by pressing the Power Button on your blender.
2. Add the pear, cinnamon, and almond milk to the blender cup.
3. Add ice cubes if you'd like it cold.
4. Press Start/Stop to blend until creamy and smooth, about 45 seconds.
5. Pour into a glass and enjoy this naturally sweet, slimming drink!

LIGHT & REFRESHING JUICES

41. Watermelon Mint Splash

Prep Time: 5 minutes | Serve: 1

Ingredients
- 1 cup watermelon cubes (seedless)
- 5–6 fresh mint leaves
- ½ cup water
- Ice cubes (optional)

Instructions
1. Press the Power Button on your Ninja Blast Portable Blender to turn it on.
2. Add the watermelon cubes, mint leaves, and water to the blender cup.
3. Add a few ice cubes if you prefer it extra cold.
4. Press Start/Stop to blend until smooth, about 30 seconds.
5. Pour into a glass, sit back, and enjoy this ultra-refreshing juice!

42. Orange Carrot Glow

Prep Time: 5 minutes | Serve: 1

Ingredients
- 1 orange, peeled and segmented
- 1 small carrot, peeled and sliced
- ½ cup water
- A few ice cubes (optional)

Instructions
1. Power on your Ninja Blast Portable Blender.
2. Add the orange, carrot, and water to the blender cup.
3. Add ice cubes for a chilled juice.
4. Press Start/Stop and blend until smooth, about 45 seconds.
5. Pour into a glass and enjoy this vibrant, glowing drink!

43. Pomegranate Punch

Prep Time: 5 minutes | Serve: 1

Ingredients
- ½ cup pomegranate seeds
- ½ cup water
- 1 tsp honey (optional)
- Ice cubes (optional)

Instructions
1. Turn on your blender by pressing the Power Button.
2. Add the pomegranate seeds, water, and honey (if you want a bit of sweetness) to the blender cup.
3. Add ice cubes if desired.
4. Press Start/Stop to blend for about 45 seconds until smooth.
5. Pour into a glass and enjoy the antioxidant-rich punch!

44. Tropical Citrus Refresh

Prep Time: 5 minutes | Serve: 1

Ingredients
- ½ orange, peeled and segmented
- ¼ cup pineapple chunks
- ½ lime, juiced
- ½ cup coconut water
- Ice cubes (optional)

Instructions
1. Press the Power Button to turn on your blender.
2. Add the orange, pineapple, lime juice, and coconut water to the blender cup.
3. Add some ice cubes if you want it chilled.
4. Press Start/Stop to blend for about 30–45 seconds.
5. Pour into a glass and feel the tropical refreshment!

45. Strawberry Lime Breeze

Prep Time: 5 minutes | Serve: 1

Ingredients
- ½ cup strawberries, hulled
- ½ lime, juiced
- ½ cup water
- Ice cubes (optional)

Instructions
1. Start by turning on your Ninja Blast Portable Blender.
2. Add the strawberries, lime juice, and water to the blender cup.
3. Add ice cubes if you prefer it extra cold.
4. Press Start/Stop and blend until smooth, about 30–45 seconds.
5. Pour into a glass and savor this tangy, sweet breeze!

46. Kiwi Cucumber Cooler

Prep Time: 5 minutes | Serve: 1

Ingredients
- 1 kiwi, peeled and sliced
- ½ cucumber, sliced
- ½ cup water
- Ice cubes (optional)

Instructions
1. Power up your blender by pressing the Power Button.
2. Add the kiwi, cucumber, and water to the blender cup.
3. Add some ice cubes if you'd like it cool and refreshing.
4. Press Start/Stop to blend until smooth, about 30 seconds.
5. Pour into a glass and enjoy the fresh, hydrating taste of this cooler!

47. Peach Lemon Spritz

Prep Time: 5 minutes | Serve: 1

Ingredients
- 1 ripe peach, pitted and sliced
- ½ lemon, juiced
- ½ cup sparkling water
- Ice cubes (optional)

Instructions
1. Turn on your Ninja Blast Portable Blender.
2. Add the peach, lemon juice, and sparkling water to the blender cup.
3. Add ice cubes for a bubbly, chilled effect.
4. Press Start/Stop to blend for about 30 seconds.
5. Pour into a glass and let the peachy, lemony spritz refresh you!

48. Apple Celery Green Juice

Prep Time: 5 minutes | Serve: 1

Ingredients
- ½ apple, cored and sliced
- 1 celery stalk, chopped
- ½ cup water
- Ice cubes (optional)

Instructions
1. Press the Power Button to turn on your Ninja Blast Portable Blender.
2. Add the apple, celery, and water to the blender cup.
3. Add a few ice cubes if you'd like it cold.
4. Press Start/Stop to blend for about 45 seconds.
5. Pour into a glass and enjoy this crisp, refreshing green juice!

49. Melon Berry Refresher

Prep Time: 5 minutes | Serve: 1

Ingredients
- ½ cup cantaloupe or honeydew melon, cubed
- ¼ cup mixed berries (blueberries, raspberries, or strawberries)
- ½ cup water
- Ice cubes (optional)

Instructions
1. Power up your Ninja Blast Portable Blender.
2. Add the melon cubes, berries, and water to the blender cup.
3. Add some ice cubes for extra chill.
4. Press Start/Stop and blend until smooth, about 30–45 seconds.
5. Pour into a glass and enjoy the delicious combo of melon and berries!

50. Cranberry Lime Zest
Prep Time: 5 minutes | Serve: 1

Ingredients
- ½ cup cranberry juice (unsweetened)
- ½ lime, juiced
- ¼ cup water
- Ice cubes (optional)

Instructions
1. Start by pressing the Power Button on your blender.
2. Add the cranberry juice, lime juice, and water to the blender cup.
3. Add ice cubes if you want it extra refreshing.
4. Press Start/Stop to blend for about 30 seconds.
5. Pour into a glass, sip, and enjoy the tangy, zesty twist!

COFFEES & LATTES

51. Iced Vanilla Latte
Prep Time: 5 minutes | Serve: 1

Ingredients
- 1 cup brewed coffee, chilled
- ½ cup milk (dairy or non-dairy)
- 1 tsp vanilla extract
- 1 tsp sugar or sweetener (optional)
- Ice cubes

Instructions
1. Power on your Ninja Blast Portable Blender by pressing the Power Button.
2. Add the chilled coffee, milk, vanilla extract, and sugar (if using) to the blender cup.
3. Add a handful of ice cubes.
4. Press Start/Stop and blend until smooth and frothy, about 30 seconds.
5. Pour into a tall glass and enjoy your homemade iced vanilla latte!

52. Mocha Coconut Blast
Prep Time: 5 minutes | Serve: 1

Ingredients
- 1 cup brewed coffee, chilled
- ½ cup coconut milk
- 1 tbsp cocoa powder
- 1 tsp sugar or sweetener (optional)
- Ice cubes

Instructions
1. Turn on your Ninja Blast by pressing the Power Button.
2. Add the coffee, coconut milk, cocoa powder, and sugar to the blender.
3. Toss in a handful of ice cubes to make it icy.
4. Press Start/Stop and blend for about 45 seconds until creamy.
5. Pour into your favorite glass, sip, and enjoy the tropical mocha flavors!

53. Cinnamon Spiced Cold Brew
Prep Time: 5 minutes | Serve: 1

Ingredients
- 1 cup cold brew coffee
- ½ cup milk (any kind)
- ¼ tsp ground cinnamon
- 1 tsp sugar or sweetener (optional)
- Ice cubes

Instructions
1. Power up your Ninja Blast Portable Blender.
2. Add the cold brew coffee, milk, cinnamon, and sugar if you'd like it sweet.
3. Add ice cubes to keep it cool and refreshing.
4. Press Start/Stop to blend for about 30 seconds.
5. Pour into a glass and savor the comforting, spiced goodness!

54. Caramel Espresso Smoothie
Prep Time: 5 minutes | Serve: 1

Ingredients
- 1 shot espresso, chilled
- ½ cup milk (dairy or non-dairy)
- 1 tbsp caramel sauce
- 1 banana, sliced
- Ice cubes

Instructions
1. Press the Power Button on your Ninja Blast Portable Blender.
2. Add the chilled espresso, milk, caramel sauce, banana, and ice cubes to the blender.
3. Press Start/Stop and blend until smooth, about 45 seconds.
4. Pour into a glass, add a drizzle of caramel on top if desired, and enjoy!

55. Pumpkin Spice Latte

Prep Time: 5 minutes | Serve: 1

Ingredients
- 1 cup brewed coffee, chilled
- ½ cup milk (dairy or non-dairy)
- 1 tbsp pumpkin puree
- ½ tsp pumpkin pie spice
- 1 tsp sugar or sweetener (optional)
- Ice cubes

Instructions
1. Turn on your Ninja Blast Portable Blender.
2. Add the coffee, milk, pumpkin puree, pumpkin pie spice, and sugar if desired.
3. Add ice cubes to chill.
4. Press Start/Stop and blend for about 45 seconds until creamy.
5. Pour into a glass and get cozy with this fall-inspired latte!

56. Almond Mocha Delight

Prep Time: 5 minutes | Serve: 1

Ingredients
- 1 cup brewed coffee, chilled
- ½ cup almond milk
- 1 tbsp cocoa powder
- 1 tsp sugar or sweetener (optional)
- Ice cubes

Instructions
1. Start by pressing the Power Button on your Ninja Blast.
2. Add the coffee, almond milk, cocoa powder, and sweetener to the blender.
3. Add a handful of ice cubes to make it nice and cold.
4. Press Start/Stop and blend until smooth, about 30 seconds.
5. Pour into your favorite glass and enjoy this almond-chocolate treat!

57. Matcha Green Tea Latte

Prep Time: 5 minutes | Serve: 1

Ingredients
- 1 tsp matcha powder
- 1 cup milk (any kind)
- 1 tsp honey or sweetener (optional)
- Ice cubes

Instructions
1. Press the Power Button to turn on your blender.
2. Add the matcha powder, milk, honey (if using), and ice cubes to the blender cup.
3. Press Start/Stop to blend until frothy and smooth, about 45 seconds.
4. Pour into a glass and enjoy this refreshing green tea latte!

58. Vanilla Almond Latte

Prep Time: 5 minutes | Serve: 1

Ingredients
- 1 cup brewed coffee, chilled
- ½ cup almond milk
- 1 tsp vanilla extract
- 1 tsp sugar or sweetener (optional)
- Ice cubes

Instructions
1. Power up your Ninja Blast by pressing the Power Button.
2. Add the coffee, almond milk, vanilla extract, and sweetener if you want a little extra sweetness.
3. Add ice cubes for a cool latte.
4. Press Start/Stop and blend for about 30 seconds.
5. Pour into a glass and enjoy the smooth, nutty vanilla flavor!

59. Classic Cold Brew

Prep Time: 5 minutes | Serve: 1

Ingredients
- 1 cup cold brew coffee
- ½ cup milk or water (for a lighter version)
- Ice cubes

Instructions
1. Turn on your Ninja Blast by pressing the Power Button.
2. Add the cold brew coffee and your choice of milk or water to the blender cup.
3. Add ice cubes to keep it icy and refreshing.
4. Press Start/Stop to blend for about 30 seconds.
5. Pour into a glass and enjoy this simple, classic cold brew!

60. Honey Cinnamon Iced Coffee

Prep Time: 5 minutes | Serve: 1

Ingredients
- 1 cup brewed coffee, chilled
- ½ cup milk (dairy or non-dairy)
- 1 tsp honey
- ¼ tsp ground cinnamon
- Ice cubes

Instructions
1. Press the Power Button to turn on your Ninja Blast.
2. Add the coffee, milk, honey, and cinnamon to the blender cup.
3. Add ice cubes to keep it cool.
4. Press Start/Stop and blend until smooth and frothy, about 30 seconds.
5. Pour into a glass and enjoy the sweet and spicy flavors of this iced coffee!

SALAD DRESSINGS

61. Classic Balsamic Vinaigrette

Prep Time: 5 minutes | Serve: 4

Ingredients
- ¼ cup balsamic vinegar
- ½ cup olive oil
- 1 tsp Dijon mustard
- 1 clove garlic, minced
- Salt and pepper, to taste

Instructions
1. Press the Power Button to turn on your Ninja Blast.
2. Add balsamic vinegar, olive oil, Dijon mustard, minced garlic, salt, and pepper to the blender cup.
3. Press Start/Stop and blend for about 20 seconds, or until well combined and smooth.
4. Taste and adjust seasoning if needed. Pour into a jar and drizzle over your favorite salad!

62. Creamy Caesar Dressing

Prep Time: 5 minutes | Serve: 4

Ingredients
- ½ cup mayonnaise
- 1 clove garlic, minced
- 1 tbsp lemon juice
- 1 tbsp Dijon mustard
- ¼ cup grated Parmesan cheese
- Salt and pepper, to taste

Instructions
1. Power on your Ninja Blast Portable Blender.
2. Add mayonnaise, minced garlic, lemon juice, Dijon mustard, Parmesan cheese, salt, and pepper to the blender cup.
3. Press Start/Stop and blend until smooth and creamy, about 20 seconds.
4. Pour over crisp romaine lettuce, sprinkle with extra Parmesan if desired, and enjoy a creamy Caesar experience!

63. Zesty Italian Dressing

Prep Time: 5 minutes | Serve: 4

Ingredients
- ¼ cup red wine vinegar
- ½ cup olive oil
- 1 tsp Italian seasoning
- ½ tsp garlic powder
- ½ tsp onion powder
- Salt and pepper, to taste

Instructions
1. Turn on your Ninja Blast by pressing the Power Button.
2. Add red wine vinegar, olive oil, Italian seasoning, garlic powder, onion powder, salt, and pepper to the blender.
3. Press Start/Stop and blend until fully mixed, about 15 seconds.
4. Pour into a bottle, shake well before each use, and drizzle over your salad for a zesty kick!

64. Greek Yogurt Ranch

Prep Time: 5 minutes | Serve: 4

Ingredients
- ½ cup Greek yogurt
- 1 tbsp lemon juice
- 1 tbsp fresh dill, chopped
- ½ tsp garlic powder
- ½ tsp onion powder
- Salt and pepper, to taste

Instructions
1. Press the Power Button to start your Ninja Blast.
2. Add Greek yogurt, lemon juice, dill, garlic powder, onion powder, salt, and pepper to the blender cup.
3. Press Start/Stop and blend until smooth, about 20 seconds.
4. Pour into a bowl, add a sprinkle of extra dill if you like, and enjoy over fresh greens or as a veggie dip!

65. Lemon Tahini Dressing

Prep Time: 5 minutes | Serve: 4

Ingredients
- ¼ cup tahini
- 2 tbsp lemon juice
- 2 tbsp water (add more for a thinner consistency)
- 1 clove garlic, minced
- Salt and pepper, to taste

Instructions
1. Power up your Ninja Blast Portable Blender.
2. Add tahini, lemon juice, water, minced garlic, salt, and pepper to the blender.
3. Press Start/Stop and blend until smooth, about 15 seconds. If too thick, add a little more water and blend again.
4. Drizzle over your salad or roasted veggies for a nutty, tangy taste!

66. Avocado Lime Dressing

Prep Time: 5 minutes | Serve: 4

Ingredients
- 1 ripe avocado, peeled and pitted
- Juice of 1 lime
- ¼ cup olive oil
- Salt and pepper, to taste
- Water, for thinning if needed

Instructions
1. Press the Power Button on your Ninja Blast.
2. Add avocado, lime juice, olive oil, salt, and pepper to the blender cup.
3. Press Start/Stop and blend until smooth. Add a bit of water if needed to reach your desired consistency.
4. Enjoy this creamy avocado dressing on any salad or as a delicious dip!

67. Honey Mustard Vinaigrette

Prep Time: 5 minutes | Serve: 4

Ingredients
- 2 tbsp honey
- 2 tbsp Dijon mustard
- ¼ cup apple cider vinegar
- ½ cup olive oil
- Salt and pepper, to taste

Instructions
1. Turn on your Ninja Blast Portable Blender.
2. Add honey, Dijon mustard, apple cider vinegar, olive oil, salt, and pepper to the blender.
3. Press Start/Stop and blend until fully combined and smooth, about 15 seconds.
4. Pour over greens or use as a marinade for a sweet and tangy twist!

68. Mango Cilantro Dressing

Prep Time: 5 minutes | Serve: 4

Ingredients
- ½ cup diced mango (fresh or frozen)
- 2 tbsp lime juice
- ¼ cup olive oil
- 1 tbsp fresh cilantro, chopped
- Salt and pepper, to taste

Instructions
1. Press the Power Button to activate your Ninja Blast.
2. Add diced mango, lime juice, olive oil, cilantro, salt, and pepper to the blender cup.
3. Press Start/Stop and blend until smooth, about 20 seconds.
4. Pour over your salad for a tropical and refreshing flavor burst!

69. Green Goddess Smoothie Dressing

Prep Time: 5 minutes | Serve: 4

Ingredients
- ½ avocado, peeled and pitted
- ¼ cup Greek yogurt
- 1 tbsp lemon juice
- 1 tbsp fresh parsley, chopped
- 1 tbsp fresh basil, chopped
- Salt and pepper, to taste

Instructions
1. Power on your Ninja Blast Portable Blender.
2. Add avocado, Greek yogurt, lemon juice, parsley, basil, salt, and pepper to the blender cup.
3. Press Start/Stop and blend until creamy and smooth, about 20 seconds.
4. Enjoy this creamy green goddess dressing over any salad, or use it as a dip!

70. Chipotle Lime Dressing

Prep Time: 5 minutes | Serve: 4

Ingredients
- 1 chipotle pepper in adobo sauce
- Juice of 1 lime
- ¼ cup Greek yogurt
- 2 tbsp olive oil
- Salt and pepper, to taste

Instructions
1. Start by pressing the Power Button on your Ninja Blast.
2. Add the chipotle pepper, lime juice, Greek yogurt, olive oil, salt, and pepper to the blender.
3. Press Start/Stop and blend until smooth and creamy, about 20 seconds.
4. Pour over your salad for a smoky, spicy, and tangy dressing!

KIDS SMOOTHIES

71. Chocolate Banana Bliss

Prep Time: 5 minutes | Serve: 2

Ingredients
- 1 ripe banana
- 1 tbsp cocoa powder
- 1 tbsp peanut butter (optional)
- 1 cup milk (or dairy-free alternative)
- 1 tsp honey or maple syrup (optional)

Instructions
1. Power on your Ninja Blast Portable Blender by pressing the Power Button.
2. Add the banana, cocoa powder, peanut butter (if using), milk, and honey or maple syrup to the blender cup.
3. Press Start/Stop and blend for about 20 seconds, or until smooth and creamy.
4. Pour into cups and serve this chocolatey treat to your little ones – they'll love it!

72. Blueberry Burst

Prep Time: 5 minutes | Serve: 2

Ingredients
- 1 cup frozen blueberries
- 1/2 banana
- 1/2 cup Greek yogurt (or dairy-free)
- 1/2 cup orange juice

Instructions
1. Turn on your Ninja Blast Portable Blender by pressing the Power Button.
2. Add the blueberries, banana, Greek yogurt, and orange juice to the blender cup.
3. Press Start/Stop and blend until smooth, about 20 seconds.
4. Pour into glasses and watch the kids enjoy the burst of blueberry goodness!

73. Strawberry Vanilla Twist

Prep Time: 5 minutes | Serve: 2

Ingredients
- 1 cup frozen strawberries
- 1/2 tsp vanilla extract
- 1/2 cup milk (or dairy-free alternative)
- 1 tbsp honey (optional)

Instructions
1. Press the Power Button to turn on the Ninja Blast.
2. Add the strawberries, vanilla extract, milk, and honey to the blender cup.
3. Press Start/Stop and blend for 15-20 seconds until smooth.
4. Pour into cups and enjoy a creamy, fruity twist!

74. Tropical Pineapple Punch

Prep Time: 5 minutes | Serve: 2

Ingredients
- 1 cup frozen pineapple chunks
- 1/2 banana
- 1/2 cup coconut milk
- 1/2 cup orange juice

Instructions
1. Power up your Ninja Blast Portable Blender by pressing the Power Button.
2. Add the pineapple chunks, banana, coconut milk, and orange juice to the blender.
3. Press Start/Stop and blend for about 20 seconds, until smooth.
4. Pour into cups and serve this tropical smoothie for a fun, fruity drink!

75. Orange Cream Dream

Prep Time: 5 minutes | Serve: 2

Ingredients
- 1 cup frozen orange segments
- 1/2 cup vanilla yogurt
- 1/4 cup orange juice
- 1/2 tsp vanilla extract

Instructions
1. Turn on your Ninja Blast Portable Blender.
2. Add the frozen orange segments, vanilla yogurt, orange juice, and vanilla extract to the blender.
3. Press Start/Stop and blend until smooth and creamy, about 20 seconds.
4. Pour into glasses and enjoy a sweet and creamy orange treat!

76. Peanut Butter Banana Pop

Prep Time: 5 minutes | Serve: 2

Ingredients
- 1 ripe banana
- 1 tbsp peanut butter
- 1/2 cup milk (or dairy-free alternative)
- 1/2 tsp honey or maple syrup (optional)

Instructions
1. Power on your Ninja Blast Portable Blender by pressing the Power Button.
2. Add the banana, peanut butter, milk, and honey or maple syrup to the blender.
3. Press Start/Stop and blend for about 20 seconds, until smooth.
4. Pour into cups and watch your kids enjoy the nutty, creamy goodness!

77. Apple Pie Smoothie

Prep Time: 5 minutes | Serve: 2

Ingredients
- 1 apple, peeled and chopped
- 1/2 banana
- 1/2 tsp cinnamon
- 1/2 cup vanilla yogurt
- 1/2 cup milk (or dairy-free alternative)

Instructions
1. Press the Power Button on your Ninja Blast Portable Blender.
2. Add the apple, banana, cinnamon, vanilla yogurt, and milk to the blender.
3. Press Start/Stop and blend for about 20 seconds, or until smooth.
4. Pour into glasses and serve this sweet, apple-pie-inspired smoothie!

78. Watermelon Wonder

Prep Time: 5 minutes | Serve: 2

Ingredients
- 1 cup watermelon cubes (frozen or fresh)
- 1/2 cup strawberries
- 1/2 cup coconut water

Instructions
1. Power up your Ninja Blast Portable Blender.
2. Add the watermelon cubes, strawberries, and coconut water to the blender cup.
3. Press Start/Stop and blend for about 15-20 seconds, until smooth.
4. Pour into cups and serve this refreshing summer treat to your kids!

79. Raspberry Lemonade Twist

Prep Time: 5 minutes | Serve: 2

Ingredients
- 1/2 cup frozen raspberries
- 1/2 banana
- Juice of 1 lemon
- 1/2 cup water or coconut water
- 1 tsp honey (optional)

Instructions
1. Turn on your Ninja Blast by pressing the Power Button.
2. Add the raspberries, banana, lemon juice, water, and honey to the blender.
3. Press Start/Stop and blend until smooth, about 20 seconds.
4. Pour into glasses and enjoy a refreshing and tangy smoothie!

80. Cherry Berry Explosion

Prep Time: 5 minutes | Serve: 2

Ingredients
- 1/2 cup frozen cherries
- 1/2 cup frozen strawberries
- 1/2 banana
- 1/2 cup almond milk (or milk of choice)
- 1 tsp honey (optional)

Instructions
1. Power on your Ninja Blast Portable Blender by pressing the Power Button.
2. Add the cherries, strawberries, banana, almond milk, and honey to the blender.
3. Press Start/Stop and blend until smooth, about 20 seconds.
4. Pour into cups and enjoy the burst of fruity flavor!

MILKSHAKES

81. Classic Vanilla Bean Milkshake

Prep Time: 5 minutes | Serve: 2

Ingredients
- 2 cups vanilla ice cream
- 1/2 cup milk (or dairy-free alternative)
- 1/2 tsp vanilla extract
- 1 tbsp sugar (optional)

Instructions
1. Turn on your Ninja Blast Portable Blender by pressing the Power Button.
2. Add the vanilla ice cream, milk, vanilla extract, and sugar to the blender.
3. Press Start/Stop and blend until smooth and creamy, about 20 seconds.
4. Pour into glasses and enjoy the classic flavor of vanilla!

82. Chocolate Fudge Milkshake

Prep Time: 5 minutes | Serve: 2

Ingredients
- 2 cups chocolate ice cream
- 1/2 cup milk (or dairy-free alternative)
- 2 tbsp chocolate syrup
- 1/4 cup chocolate fudge (optional for extra decadence)

Instructions
1. Press the Power Button to turn on your Ninja Blast Portable Blender.
2. Add the chocolate ice cream, milk, chocolate syrup, and chocolate fudge (if using) to the blender.
3. Press Start/Stop and blend for about 20 seconds, until smooth.
4. Pour into glasses and drizzle with more chocolate syrup if you're feeling fancy!

83. Peanut Butter Cup Shake

Prep Time: 5 minutes | Serve: 2

Ingredients
- 2 cups vanilla ice cream
- 1/4 cup peanut butter
- 1/2 cup milk (or dairy-free alternative)
- 2 tbsp chocolate syrup

Instructions
1. Turn on the Ninja Blast Portable Blender by pressing the Power Button.
2. Add the vanilla ice cream, peanut butter, milk, and chocolate syrup to the blender.
3. Press Start/Stop and blend until smooth and creamy, about 20 seconds.
4. Pour into glasses and top with crushed peanuts for a fun crunch!

84. Cookies & Cream Delight

Prep Time: 5 minutes | Serve: 2

Ingredients
- 2 cups cookies and cream ice cream
- 1/2 cup milk (or dairy-free alternative)
- 2-3 crushed chocolate sandwich cookies (for extra crunch)

Instructions
1. Power on your Ninja Blast Portable Blender by pressing the Power Button.
2. Add the cookies and cream ice cream, milk, and crushed cookies to the blender.
3. Press Start/Stop and blend until smooth, about 20 seconds.
4. Pour into cups and garnish with more crushed cookies on top!

85. Strawberry Cheesecake Shake

Prep Time: 5 minutes | Serve: 2

Ingredients
- 2 cups strawberry ice cream
- 1/2 cup cream cheese (softened)
- 1/2 cup milk (or dairy-free alternative)
- 1 tbsp graham cracker crumbs (for that cheesecake crust vibe)

Instructions
1. Turn on your Ninja Blast Portable Blender by pressing the Power Button.
2. Add the strawberry ice cream, cream cheese, milk, and graham cracker crumbs to the blender.
3. Press Start/Stop and blend until smooth and creamy, about 20 seconds.
4. Pour into glasses and top with more graham cracker crumbs or fresh strawberries.

86. Salted Caramel Crunch

Prep Time: 5 minutes | Serve: 2

Ingredients
- 2 cups vanilla ice cream
- 1/4 cup salted caramel sauce
- 1/2 cup milk (or dairy-free alternative)
- 1/4 cup crushed pretzels (for crunch)

Instructions
1. Press the Power Button to turn on the Ninja Blast Portable Blender.
2. Add the vanilla ice cream, salted caramel sauce, milk, and crushed pretzels to the blender.
3. Press Start/Stop and blend for about 20 seconds, until smooth and creamy.
4. Pour into glasses and drizzle with extra caramel sauce for an extra treat!

87. Mint Chocolate Chip Shake

Prep Time: 5 minutes | Serve: 2

Ingredients
- 2 cups mint chocolate chip ice cream
- 1/2 cup milk (or dairy-free alternative)
- 1/4 cup chocolate chips

Instructions
1. Turn on your Ninja Blast Portable Blender by pressing the Power Button.
2. Add the mint chocolate chip ice cream, milk, and chocolate chips to the blender.
3. Press Start/Stop and blend until smooth, about 20 seconds.
4. Pour into cups and garnish with extra chocolate chips or a sprig of mint!

88. Banana Split Milkshake

Prep Time: 5 minutes | Serve: 2

Ingredients
- 1 cup vanilla ice cream
- 1 cup strawberry ice cream
- 1 ripe banana (sliced)
- 1/2 cup milk (or dairy-free alternative)
- Whipped cream and cherry (optional for topping)

Instructions
1. Press the Power Button to power on your Ninja Blast.
2. Add the vanilla ice cream, strawberry ice cream, banana, and milk to the blender.
3. Press Start/Stop and blend until smooth, about 20 seconds.
4. Pour into glasses, top with whipped cream and a cherry, and serve!

89. Pistachio Dream Shake

Prep Time: 5 minutes | Serve: 2

Ingredients
- 2 cups pistachio ice cream
- 1/2 cup milk (or dairy-free alternative)
- 1 tbsp honey (optional)

Instructions
1. Turn on your Ninja Blast Portable Blender by pressing the Power Button.
2. Add the pistachio ice cream, milk, and honey to the blender.
3. Press Start/Stop and blend for about 20 seconds, until smooth.
4. Pour into glasses and enjoy a nutty, creamy shake!

90. Espresso Brownie Blast

Prep Time: 5 minutes | Serve: 2

Ingredients
- 2 cups coffee ice cream
- 1/4 cup brewed espresso (cooled)
- 1 tbsp chocolate syrup
- 1/4 cup brownie chunks

Instructions
1. Press the Power Button to turn on your Ninja Blast Portable Blender.
2. Add the coffee ice cream, brewed espresso, chocolate syrup, and brownie chunks to the blender.
3. Press Start/Stop and blend for 20 seconds, until smooth and creamy.
4. Pour into glasses and top with extra brownie chunks for a chocolatey finish!

BABY FOOD

91. Banana Pear Puree

Prep Time: 5 minutes | Serve: 2

Ingredients
- 1 ripe banana
- 1 ripe pear, peeled and chopped
- 1-2 tbsp water (or breast milk/formula)

Instructions
1. Press the Power Button to turn on your Ninja Blast Portable Blender.
2. Add the banana and chopped pear into the blender.
3. Add a little water (or breast milk/formula) to reach a smooth consistency.
4. Press Start/Stop and blend until completely smooth, about 20-30 seconds.
5. Pour into a bowl and serve!

92. Sweet Potato Carrot Mash

Prep Time: 10 minutes | Serve: 2

Ingredients
- 1 small sweet potato, peeled and chopped
- 1 small carrot, peeled and chopped
- 2 tbsp water (or breast milk/formula)

Instructions
1. Steam the sweet potato and carrot until tender, about 10-15 minutes.
2. Turn on your Ninja Blast Portable Blender by pressing the Power Button.
3. Add the steamed sweet potato and carrot to the blender.
4. Add water (or breast milk/formula) to help blend into a smooth puree.
5. Press Start/Stop and blend for about 20 seconds, until smooth.
6. Serve warm and enjoy!

93. Apple Avocado Smoothie

Prep Time: 5 minutes | Serve: 2

Ingredients
- 1 small apple, peeled and chopped
- 1/2 ripe avocado
- 2 tbsp water (or breast milk/formula)

Instructions
1. Press the Power Button to start your Ninja Blast Portable Blender.
2. Add the chopped apple and half an avocado to the blender.
3. Add water (or breast milk/formula) to help with blending.
4. Press Start/Stop and blend until creamy and smooth, about 20-30 seconds.
5. Pour into a bowl and serve!

94. Peach Mango Puree

Prep Time: 5 minutes | Serve: 2

Ingredients
- 1 ripe peach, peeled and chopped
- 1/2 ripe mango, peeled and chopped
- 1-2 tbsp water (or breast milk/formula)

Instructions
1. Turn on your Ninja Blast Portable Blender by pressing the Power Button.
2. Add the chopped peach and mango into the blender.
3. Add water (or breast milk/formula) to help the puree blend easily.
4. Press Start/Stop and blend until smooth and creamy, about 20 seconds.
5. Pour into a bowl and serve immediately!

95. Butternut Squash Delight

Prep Time: 10 minutes | Serve: 2

Ingredients
- 1 small butternut squash, peeled and chopped
- 2 tbsp water (or breast milk/formula)

Instructions
1. Steam or roast the butternut squash until tender, about 15-20 minutes.
2. Turn on your Ninja Blast Portable Blender by pressing the Power Button.
3. Add the cooked squash to the blender.
4. Add water (or breast milk/formula) to get a nice smooth consistency.
5. Press Start/Stop and blend until smooth, about 20-30 seconds.
6. Pour into a bowl and serve warm.

96. Carrot Spinach Blend

Prep Time: 10 minutes | Serve: 2

Ingredients
- 1 small carrot, peeled and chopped
- 1/2 cup fresh spinach
- 2 tbsp water (or breast milk/formula)

Instructions
1. Steam the carrot until tender, about 10 minutes.
2. Turn on your Ninja Blast Portable Blender by pressing the Power Button.
3. Add the steamed carrot and fresh spinach to the blender.
4. Add water (or breast milk/formula) to help it blend smoothly.
5. Press Start/Stop and blend for about 20 seconds until smooth.
6. Serve in a bowl and let your little one enjoy!

97. Blueberry Oatmeal Puree

Prep Time: 5 minutes | Serve: 2

Ingredients
- 1/2 cup blueberries (fresh or frozen)
- 1/4 cup cooked oatmeal
- 2 tbsp water (or breast milk/formula)

Instructions
1. Turn on your Ninja Blast Portable Blender by pressing the Power Button.
2. Add the blueberries and cooked oatmeal to the blender.
3. Add water (or breast milk/formula) to help blend everything smoothly.
4. Press Start/Stop and blend for 20 seconds, until smooth.
5. Serve in a bowl and enjoy!

98. Pea & Pear Puree

Prep Time: 5 minutes | Serve: 2

Ingredients
- 1/2 cup peas (fresh or frozen)
- 1 ripe pear, peeled and chopped
- 1-2 tbsp water (or breast milk/formula)

Instructions
1. Steam the peas until soft, about 5-7 minutes.
2. Turn on your Ninja Blast Portable Blender by pressing the Power Button.
3. Add the peas and chopped pear to the blender.
4. Add water (or breast milk/formula) to blend smoothly.
5. Press Start/Stop and blend until smooth and creamy, about 20 seconds.
6. Serve and enjoy!

99. Mango & Banana Bliss

Prep Time: 5 minutes | Serve: 2

Ingredients
- 1/2 ripe mango, peeled and chopped
- 1 ripe banana
- 1-2 tbsp water (or breast milk/formula)

Instructions
1. Turn on the Ninja Blast Portable Blender by pressing the Power Button.
2. Add the chopped mango and banana to the blender.
3. Add water (or breast milk/formula) to help blend the ingredients.
4. Press Start/Stop and blend until smooth and creamy, about 20 seconds.
5. Pour into a bowl and serve!

100. Zucchini & Apple Mix

Prep Time: 5 minutes | Serve: 2

Ingredients
- 1 small zucchini, peeled and chopped
- 1 small apple, peeled and chopped
- 2 tbsp water (or breast milk/formula)

Instructions
1. Steam the zucchini until soft, about 5 minutes.
2. Turn on your Ninja Blast Portable Blender by pressing the Power Button.
3. Add the steamed zucchini and chopped apple to the blender.
4. Add water (or breast milk/formula) to help blend it into a smooth puree.
5. Press Start/Stop and blend until smooth, about 20 seconds.
6. Serve warm and enjoy!

101. Sweet Potato Pumpkin Mash

Prep Time: 10 minutes | Serve: 2

Ingredients
- 1 small sweet potato, peeled and chopped
- 1/2 cup canned pumpkin puree
- 2 tbsp water (or breast milk/formula)

Instructions
1. Steam or roast the sweet potato until tender, about 10-15 minutes.
2. Turn on the Ninja Blast Portable Blender by pressing the Power Button.
3. Add the sweet potato and pumpkin puree to the blender.
4. Add water (or breast milk/formula) to achieve a smooth texture.
5. Press Start/Stop and blend for about 20 seconds.
6. Serve warm and enjoy!

Printed in Great Britain
by Amazon